LIFE, LAUGHTER, AND THE PURSUIT OF SARCASM

DAN ADAMCHAK

NEWMAN SPRINGS PUBLISHING
320 Broad Street
Red Bank, NJ 07701

First originally published by Newman
Springs Publishing 2024

ISBN 979-8-89308-702-4 (Paperback)
ISBN 979-8-89308-703-1 (Digital)

Printed in the United States of America

To any and all people that need to laugh as well as all the people who unknowingly helped me hone my sarcastic skills

Contents

Preface

The reason behind this book is to show humor can be found in nearly everything. I've worked in the customer service industry for more than twenty years, so needless to say, I have witnessed a lot that have entitled, ignorant, and arrogant people in their natural environment. It's thanks to these people that I have been able to sharpen my sarcasm. It was only recently though that some coworkers convinced me to start writing down the comments to keep them for future laughter. I've decided to break this book into sections based on whether the comment is off the top of my head, a cliché kind of remark, a mix of lines from the entertainment industry, and even some profound lines to make you think.

Introduction

So we know they say that humans have five major senses: taste, touch, sight, smell, and hearing. While we can survive without some of these—that is, sight and hearing—there is one sense necessary for survival, a sense of humor. While the majority of these comments are from the inner workings of my brain, not all of them are. For those that are not mine, I have given credit where is due. On the off chance that a comment is not mine and I don't credit the origin, I apologize as I do not know who originally said aforementioned comment.

Off the Top of My Head

There isn't going to be any sense of order to these remarks because every day at work, I encounter different types of people. Whether my blood sugar was low, they were in a bad mood, or any number of things, the actions of the customers, management, or even coworkers seemed to bring out my inner smart-ass.

Live, laugh, and laugh some more.

When all else fails, open a bottle of wine.

Some things you just can't unsee though you wish you could.

The computer is only as smart as the person who programs it.

Common sense isn't very common anymore.

If at first you didn't succeed, just pray no one saw you fail.

How are we expected to succeed when management consistently fails us?

Stupidity is more common than common sense.

The most underappreciated jobs are usually the most important.

I'm not sure which is worse, monotony or stupidity.

Stupidity doesn't discriminate; it comes in all shapes and sizes.

It's a good thing stupidity isn't contagious. Management wouldn't like that much competition.

Just remember, you can't spell bureaucrats without BS.

The power of observation is so rare it should be considered a superpower.

The level of ineptitude is astounding.

Just when you thought the idiocy couldn't get any worse, they surprise you.

Of course, I talk to myself; I need to have an intelligent conversation every now and then.

I would say that I work with idiots, but that would give idiots a bad name.

Why should I ignore the voices in my head? That's where some of my best ideas come from.

Of course, I'm serious, a serious smart-ass.

I just need to win either the Powerball jackpot or Publisher's Clearinghouse without playing. Is that asking too much?

Keep your friends close, your enemies closer, and your coworkers at arm's length.

When in doubt, blame management.

Just remember, when push comes to shove, management won't hesitate to throw you under the bus to save their own skin.

This place thrives on Murphy's law.

Management is very much profit over people-oriented.

Not sure which is harder to deal with, entitled customers or incompetent management.

It seems the more incompetent a person, the higher up the corporate ladder they can go.

It's pretty bad when one of the best things about your job is the music playing over the PA system.

Just another unnecessary step in this bullshit process.

A three-ring circus being run by a blind monkey.

I thought this level of ineptitude was reserved for government use only.

I gamble with my life, not my money.

They usually say, where there's smoke, there's fire; around here, where there's smoke, there's someone thinking.

Monkey see, monkey do, monkey get in trouble too.

Do as I say, not as I do.

It's only illegal if you get caught.

The police, never there when you need them, always there when you don't.

A friend of mine once said that pain is the only true feeling that lets you know you're alive.

I see all, I know nothing.

When push comes to shove, surprise them with a left hook.

He who laughs loudest usually didn't get the joke.

Whoever came up with the saying that there are no stupid questions has obviously never worked in customer service.

We should remove the warning labels and let natural selection run its course.

The ones that are the most clueless are usually the ones most adamant that they know what they are talking about.

Of course, I'm a smart-ass; some part of me has to be smart.

Why is there a highway to hell but only a stairway to heaven?

I have never stolen a thing in my life, permanently borrowed sure, but never stolen.

It's all fun and games until someone loses an eye, then it's downright hilarious.

I'm happier than a prankster on April Fool's Day.

The best place to hide things is in plain sight.

Just remember, you're not as important as you think you are.

I try not to think; it gets me in trouble.

Of all the things I've lost, I miss my mind the most, but my sanity is a close second, and my virginity is a distant third.

Two wrongs don't make a right, but three lefts do.

When someone says "I'll be right back," respond with "Thanks for the warning."

If this job looks so easy, you're more than welcome to try.

Not the brightest bulb in the chandelier.

A few sandwiches short of a picnic.

Not the sharpest tool in the shed.

Common decency and respect for others seems to disappear at buffets.

Strong back, weak mind.

Sarcasm is a true art form.

Your elevator doesn't go all the way to the top floor, does it?

I refuse to do a battle of wits with an unarmed man.

Looking for sympathy? It's in the dictionary between shit and syphilis.

This place brings out the smart-ass in me.

Your village called; they want their idiot back.

Ever wonder if the village idiot and the town drunk are the same person?

Mind games are my favorite kind of games to play.

This place takes control out of controlled chaos.

To say I work with idiots would be an understatement.

Nothing like cornering an employee just so you can stroke your ego.

This place thrives on inconsistency.

Consistently inconsistent.

Need to buy these people the board game Clue, at least then they can honestly have a clue.

If they worried about the employees as much as they do their image, it would be a good place to work.

Everyone is so busy shifting blame around that there is no accountability.

When you assume, you make an ass out of you and me.

Sarcasm, it's what I do best.

This level of idiocy should be illegal.

This place is just the blind leading the blind.

Taking ignorance is bliss to a whole other level.

There are so many hoops to through, I could be a gymnast.

I came, I saw, I made a sarcastic remark.

I thrive on caffeine, wine, and sarcasm.

I came, I saw, I went to the bar.

They said I could be anything, so I became sarcastic.

Sarcasm, just another service I offer.

My sarcasm is one of my most endearing traits.

Happy people scare me; it's not natural to be that happy.

It's the quiet people that you need to worry about.

Wow! You're a special kind of stupid, aren't you?

My ass is the smartest part of me.

I'm not as stupid as you look.

Too much shit and not enough room.

Some people have more dollars than sense.

The lack of communication is astounding.

I may be crazy, but I'm not stupid.

If you can't dazzle them with knowledge, baffle them with bullshit.

If I had a dollar for every stupid question I've been asked, I could retire tomorrow.

I believe half of what I hear and none of what I say.

A family business being run by a dysfunctional family.

People need to check their entitlement at the door.

No, I don't know who you are. Do you know who I am?

Some people like playing board games; others like video games—personally, I prefer mind games.

I think clown college is the alma mater of a lot of business executives.

A dinner without wine is like a day without sunshine.

Is it just me or does Jeff Bezos look like Lex Luthor?

Someday this place is going to be the punch line of a comedy routine.

Life is too short to be serious.

Learn to laugh so you can learn to live.

Above all else, learn to laugh at yourself before you laugh at others.

Contrary to popular belief, the customer is not always right.

You can't argue with stupid; you'll never win.

The only person who likes an ass-kisser is the one whose ass is being kissed.

Sarcasm is my superpower; stupid people are my kryptonite.

I don't usually think before I speak; I like to surprise myself with my response.

Life, liberty, and the pursuit of laughter.

So many unnecessary steps on the path to progress.

It's a good thing some foods don't taste as bad as they smell.

The more pompous you are, the less effort it takes to make you look like a fool.

Contrary to popular belief, failure is always an option.

If R2-D2 was a good guy, how come they bleeped out everything he said.

I don't care what other people say, cartoons are written on two different levels.

People say so many things taste like chicken; who's to say that it isn't chicken that tastes like something else?

I'm allergic to stupid people; I break out in fits of sarcasm.

When everything is all said and done, laughter will persevere.

If a person starts a statement with "I mean no disrespect," be prepared to be disrespected.

Never underestimate the power of stupidity.

I have a much higher tolerance of pain than I do for stupidity.

If you ask for an honest opinion, be ready to be offended.

Unless you have a foot fetish, quit putting your foot in your mouth.

Some people would be better off if they heeded their own advice.

Silence is boring, sarcasm is fun.

If a known smart-ass is quiet, be warned and proceed with caution.

If you ever question whether or not your parents have a sense of humor, just look in the mirror.

Never underestimate the power of laughter.

A sarcastic mind is a terrible thing to silence.

Sarcasm is an art that few have mastered.

Pretending to work is usually harder than actually working.

'Tis better to have cracked a joke and nobody laughed than to have never joked at all.

All work and no play give you a dull sense of humor.

A life without humor is a life of despair.

Never mind "kill them with kindness," "slay them with sarcasm."

Ignorance is bliss explains why so many people are happy.

Comedic timing is a gift.

Sleep is overrated.

If you're going to ask me a question, at least wait till I answer before you walk away ignoring me.

The public's acceptance of people wearing pajamas everywhere they go is disturbing.

Just when I thought the questions couldn't get any dumber, someone surprised me.

Ever look around and wonder who has a body buried in their backyard?

Customer service employees should be allowed to smack one customer a day.

An important sense that seems to allude most people is fashion sense.

Live to laugh, laugh to live.

I feel like smartphones are actually making people dumber.

When my mind wanders, I worry that it might not come back.

Imagination…something not enough people use.

Patience is a virtue that few people possess.

Life has a fine line between normal and crazy, and I trip over it on a daily basis.

Reality is an uneven playing field that too many people occupy.

I want a real check, not a reality check.

Alongside the food I cook all day, I usually tend to cook up some trouble as well.

The best customers are the ones who know what they want and don't talk to me.

Sometimes I just need a fortress of solitude and a bottle of wine.

The less deserving of a leadership role a person is, the more likely they are to obtain it.

The ego is like a balloon in that it can be inflated and deflated with relative ease.

It's not the fast pace of life that worries me, it's the sudden stop at the end.

Some people are so good at playing dumb. I wonder if they're really playing or are they just really that dumb.

Instead of the proverbial nail, how about we hit an entitled person on the head?

Sometimes being lost in the fog can be a good thing.

Some days you just wake up and know it's going to be a bad day.

Sometimes the good guy just needs to lose.

Why pay to see animals in captivity at the zoo when you can work retail and see them in their natural environment?

Why does the full moon seem to bring out the crazy?

Sure, inner peace would be nice, but so would a few million dollars.

Do I like my job? No, but do I feel valued as an employee? Also no.

Let's be real with ourselves…there will never be world peace; we can't even agree which side of the road to drive on.

One man's wife is another man's mistress.

People who think staring at me will make me move faster don't know how petty I can be.

Sarcasm is like force; you must let it flow through you.

Don't look at me in that tone of voice.

The key to a successful marriage is to work different shifts. The less you see each other, the fewer chances you have to argue.

You do it your way; I'll do it the right way.

Sarcastic remarks are like a burp, you just need to let them happen.

Getting in the way is what most people seem to be best at.

I'm an irresponsible smart-ass…I don't hold back or filter the remarks I make.

Stop signs with a white border are optional.

When it comes to traffic lights, red means stop, green means go, and yellow means go faster.

The stupid questions never cease to amaze me.

There aren't enough available brains to feed the zombies if and when the zombie apocalypse happens.

For every stupid question I receive, I lose a little bit more hope for humanity…there isn't much left.

If at first you don't succeed, go have a drink and forget about it.

If wine is the elixir of life, sarcasm is the grapes.

The mind works in mysterious ways, especially mine.

I bet the highway to hell is an eight-lane road that has to merge down to one lane.

I wonder if the stairway to heaven is an escalator.

The idea of being alone with my thoughts scares me.

Another day, another smart-ass remark.

I wish people would worry about themselves as much as they worry about things beyond their control.

The way some people prioritize things is mind-boggling.

Not sure which is worse, an entitled trophy wife or a passive-aggressive Karen.

So many ignorant people are so blissfully unaware.

A day with no sarcasm is a day I dread.

This place is the circus, and I'm the sideshow.

Those at fault are the same ones least likely to admit it.

With so many politicians talking out of their asses, I'm surprised DC doesn't smell like an outhouse.

Sarcasm is like chicken pox, not everyone gets it.

Enough with the pumpkin spice already! What's next, pumpkin spice edible underwear?

If no one sees it happen, did it even happen?

Do cars with LED headlights really need a high beam setting?

Of all the sounds out there, I like the sound of silence best of all.

We should be able to bill a doctor for the time we spend waiting for them.

Laughter is like the fountain of youth; the more you laugh, the younger you feel.

They need to bring back Hammurabi's law.

Why does the American culture value athletes over teachers, first responders, nurses, and soldiers?

If no one understands a sarcastic remark, does the remark maker get a redo?

Sarcasm is like an ancient language that very few people understand. I sympathize with those who don't.

Cats are like teenagers, they only come to you when they want something.

Dogs are like toddlers, easily amused by the simplest of things.

Cats can adjust their ears so that a human voice goes in one and out the other.

Wine a little, you'll feel better.

Pretty disturbing how the side effects of some of these new medicines are worse than what they are supposed to be treating.

If both parents are sarcastic, do the sarcasm genes cancel each other out?

Maybe it's just the Gen Xer in me, but today's music just doesn't hold a candle to the music of the older generations.

This may be unpopular, but retail should wait till after Thanksgiving before advertising Christmas.

Why do people who sit in an office all day with no public interaction have to dress up for work?

Do you really need to FaceTime or have your phone on speaker? The rest of the public don't want to hear your entire conversation.

Is it just me or do the bad guys always seem to have the better of everything?

Listening to Yoda while drunk must be very confusing.

I wonder how many sadists started out as physical therapists.

Can a person without a soul have a soulmate? Asking for a friend.

Why do I scan a QR code to check in at the doctor's office?

What do you call a room full of idiots? Government.

At what age do kids start to realize that their parents aren't stupid? 'Cause it's not eighteen and twenty-two.

Yoga instructors are just physical therapists without the physical contact.

If being sarcastic is wrong, I don't want to be right.

Is it just me or should medical students have to take a handwriting course during medical school?

I'm more than content with spending the majority of my day either by myself or with my dogs.

I stopped being a people person when I encountered people.

Sometimes solitary confinement sounds appealing.

Imagine being an archeologist, getting paid to play in the dirt.

If dreaming is believing, I don't want to wake up.

I wonder how they come up with the names of these prescription drugs they advertise…do they play a game of darts?

Expect the unexpected, especially from a smart-ass.

What's the difference between partly cloudy and mostly sunny?

I have a T-shirt that says, "lost in thought, a deep, dark unfamiliar place."

You start out thinking life is a beach, but then you realize it's actually a giant litterbox filled with crap.

It's really annoying how the good guys always seem so gullible.

The bigger the ego, the less room there is for a brain.

Having young kids at Christmas is like working in a corporate setting…you do all the work and a fat guy in a suit gets all the credit.

Birthdays, the more you have, the less you celebrate.

Is there such a thing as good pain?

Don't eat yellow snow.

A known smart-ass is a force to be reckoned with.

Remember, the light at the end of the tunnel may be a train speeding toward you.

If you have to proclaim "I was joking," you're already in trouble and may as well head straight to HR.

If I have to explain a joke, there is no hope for you.

Separation anxiety sounds like something Siamese twins should get, not dogs.

When life gets you down, kick back, relax with a glass of wine, and say, "Fuck it."

Have another drink; there's always tomorrow.

The more brazen the crime, the more oblivious the criminal is.

The funnier the joke, the less politically correct it tends to be.

Karma's a bitch, and she'll get you when you least expect it.

Make sure whoever is watching your back doesn't have a knife.

Why is it that though vacations are meant to be relaxing, they rarely are?

A conundrum wrapped around an enigma.

Why does it seem the more politically correct a statement is made, the more offensive it becomes.

It almost always sounds better in your head.

If I say I don't want to go somewhere, it's nothing against the location, it's because people will be there.

Malicious compliance, oh…you mean do as I say, not as I do.

The dumber the question, the more often it is asked.

The most childish behavior I've witnessed has come from adults.

Why are nonparents so eager to give parenting advice?

Too many people don't think before they speak, yet they should.

Why do the simplest of tasks seem to take the longest to complete?

Isn't it management's job to step up if someone calls out instead of just passing the job along to someone else?

These days, you can't say anything without offending someone.

Imagine how much less road rage there would be if people would just use turn signals.

Valentine's Day is just a holiday made up in a conspiracy between the flower, greeting card, and candy industries. Otherwise, there is no way for them to make money between Christmas and Easter.

No one talks to others anymore; everything seems to be done through email or text messages.

At least 50 percent of a customer's questions would be answered if they just read the labels.

Sometimes the only fun you can have in retail is to commiserate with other workers about the customers.

There is no need for everything to have a touch screen.

Leave it too sticker to prove a nonstick pan a liar.

Sometimes holding your tongue is the most difficult task, both physically and metaphorically.

Few people can walk the walk, but even fewer can talk the talk.

Never let your mind wander, it might not come back.

If what happens in Vegas stays in Vegas, doesn't that make it Satan's waiting room?

For a memorable funeral, get someone to dress as the grim reaper and then randomly point at people throughout the service.

The world needs a good, old-fashioned toga party.

Please don't ask me what's on my mind. I have no control over what goes on in there.

It's a lawless land inside my head.

Sarcasm is to me what peanut butter is to jelly. The perfect match.

Please don't leave me alone with my thoughts. That idea scares me.

Gravity keeps me grounded.

The world is a gifted place if you make mischief a talent.

Sarcasm is an art form, and the world is the canvas.

How many times do you have to knock on heaven's door before they answer?

I wonder if there is a secret knock for heaven's door.

People working in customer service should get paid extra to compensate for all the stupid questions.

Why is it when you want the day to go by fast, it drags on for what feels like an eternity?

Trying to keep the workplace organized is like trying to clean up during a tornado.

When I'm told I can't go shopping but have to stay at home with the dogs, I'm not feeling punished, I'm ecstatic.

If by punishment you mean I get to avoid people, then I'm a glutton for punishment.

Thanks to Bluetooth, a lot of people look like they are talking to themselves.

I know the say never trust a skinny chef, but it should be more like never trust a chef without any scars or burns.

After my knee surgery, every day is leg day.

The term "booby trap" sounds a lot more explicit than it really is.

The more people at a location, the less incentive there is to go.

Why does the thirty-minute lunch break feel like it only lasts five minutes?

I love it when the toilets with sensors flush while still in use.

I wonder if toothpaste companies survey the same dentists each time they advertise a new product.

Toddlers and politicians are both very good at asking the most absurd questions.

Some of these touch screens are so sensitive. You breathe too hard within a one-foot radius and it thinks you touched it.

All rotisserie chickens are roast chickens, but not all roast chickens are rotisserie chickens.

Why is the most inconvenient spot to stand always the most popular?

It's not that I'm antisocial, it's that I'm anti-stupid people.

We should be allowed to smack parents that can't or won't control their kids in public.

Age is just a number. I may not like the number, but it's still just a number.

I categorize a lot of things as "not my problem," and frankly, I'm okay with that.

Sure, most people are good at their jobs, but then you've got others that are only good at getting in the way.

The less I see of the boss, the better I feel.

Any day above ground is a good day unless you're a subterranean animal like a naked mole rat.

If yawning is contagious, why isn't the whole world tired?

Hot and cold are relative terms.

It's not that I'm voting for one candidate; it's that I'm voting against the other one.

Correctional officers are paid to babysit and play hide and seek.

I put the fun in fundamentally flawed.

There's a method to the madness; it may be convoluted, but there's still a method.

At one point weren't all theories conspiracy theories?

Why be normal when you can be eccentric?

Management never orders what you need, always orders what you don't.

Sometimes a good one-liner can speak volumes.

Saying nothing may sometimes be the best course of action.

If a picture is worth a thousand words, what's the value of a sarcastic remark?

They say a mind is a terrible thing to waste, but what about a sense of humor?

Life is like a Rubik's Cube, with thousands of possibilities but only one winning combination.

You call it a panic room, I call it a wine cellar; deep down, we both know it's the same thing.

The term undead has been around for so long it was only a matter of time before they coined the term unalive.

I'm not short, I'm vertically challenged.

Smart-ass—sarcastically adept.

Teenager, garbage disposal—same thing really.

I'm more of a dog person than a people person.

Public shaming should be brought back into the mainstream. Maybe then some parents would learn to control their kids.

Sarcasm brings laughter and chaos to an otherwise dull world.

Sarcasm is like the spiked punch at a party, nobody knows it's there, and the next thing you know, everybody's laughing.

A good sarcastic remark is like a fine wine, you just want to savor it for a minute before you do anything else.

Thinking is something that not enough people do, but the ones that do, do it too much.

Sometimes admitting fault can be the hardest thing.

Blame is the easiest thing to pass along.

Sometimes gravity works a little too well.

Looks aren't the only thing that can be deceiving.

There is such a thing as too much too soon.

"They" already watch everything we do, what's next?

I'd rather be sarcastic than philosophical.

My luck is so bad that when my ship does come in, it's going to be the *Titanic*.

Certain types of people are much better than others at bringing out the inner cynic in me.

The unhealthier the food, the bigger (pun intended) fan base it has.

The best part about going to work is knowing you eventually get to go home.

Sarcasm is like chicken soup, even a small amount will do you good.

That's like trying to fit 10 lbs. of shit in a 5 lb. bag.

The stupidity of mankind will never cease to amaze me.

I think therefore it hurts.

Working in a grocery store, I feel like my families own personal Instacart shopper.

With as courteous as Canadians are, it's no wonder that the Canadian geese come to the United States.

The more asinine a procedure, the more adamant a company will be about following it.

In the corporate world, a simple answer is as elusive as bigfoot.

I may not have liked being in the Cub Scouts, but their "Be prepared" motto definitely prepared me for the food service industry.

Sometimes life feels like an inside joke, but I'm on the outside looking in.

If you ever feel useless, just remember they have lifeguards at the Olympic swimming events.

I may not always be right, but I'm never wrong.

Kind of ironic, the place I like the least produces some of my best sarcastic remarks.

When poet John Lydgate came up with "You can please some of the people all of the time, you can please all of the people some of the time, but you can't please all of the people all of the time," he must have been working in customer service.

If women can wear capris and skirts to work, why can't men wear shorts?

Not very reassuring that diabetes has "die" in the name.

Where's the fun in watching a YouTube channel of someone playing a game instead of playing the game yourself?

On a Disneyland ride back in the '80s, I saw a sign that said, "I see all, I know nothing."

One of my favorite shirts says, "How am I supposed to think outside of the box, they won't even let me out."

Why do all the big dogs think they're lap dogs?

There is absolutely nothing funny about hitting the funny bone.

I have nothing to do and all the time in the world to get it done.

Inevitably, the quicker you want something done, the longer it takes.

With auto-flushing toilets flushing at the slightest of movement, how are they saving water?

What do people have against using their headlights when it's raining?

If car companies can make self-driving cars, why can't they make headlights that come on when you turn the wipers on?

Why do pickup trucks and sport cars think when it's raining is the best time to try and race?

Whoever says "size doesn't matter" has obviously never been to Texas.

Why does the caffeine from coffee seem to hit different than the caffeine from soda?

A lot of the protest songs from the '60s seems to be gaining relevance again.

Driver's ed instructors are extremely brave people.

I bet a fiddle of gold would sound terrible.

How is it that Pandora can lose connectivity to the point it won't play music but can still play advertisements?

I wonder if a musician considers it an honor if "weird" AI parodies a song of theirs.

The fact that the US Navy has the second largest air force in the world is a little disconcerting.

The less dramatic the day, the better I feel.

How am I supposed to watch my eyes?

Why do we drive on parkways and park on driveways?

Why is there braille at drive-up ATMs?

Band-Aid should be the name for the people who travel and work with bands instead of roadie.

Sometimes the easiest way to confuse someone is to ask them the simplest of questions.

Why hold out for what's best when you could settle for mediocrity?

What's the point in suspenders if you're already wearing a belt or vice versa?

Sorry, Airbnb, I'll stay somewhere that doesn't ask me to clean the whole place and then still charge me an additional cleaning fee.

Is coffee considered an energy drink?

You supply the wine; I'll supply the laughter.

What's the bigger scam, government or religion?

I wonder how Roald would feel knowing a politician is trying to imitate the Oompa Loompas.

Another day another one dollar before taxes.

Why wear shorts if you're going to also wear a winter coat?

I wonder how many people confuse baklava with balaclava.

They say you learn something new every day. Whether it's a good thing or not is yet to be determined.

I'm only sarcastic on days that with a y.

They say time flies when you're having fun; it's no wonder the workday lasts so long.

If it weren't for my sarcasm, I think I would have had an existential crisis by now.

I don't know which would be worse, being with a group of obnoxious people or being alone with my thoughts.

If I were paid to think, they wouldn't like the results.

An endless cycle of stupidity.

It's not that I dropped something, I'm just making sure gravity still works.

In Texas, both BBQ and football are both considered religions.

Who determined that batshit is crazy?

Why ask employees what their preferred shift is if you're just going to ignore the response?

The workplace seems to thrive on neglect and Murphy's law.

Another day, another headache.

Seasonal depression, seasonal allergies…is there anything seasonal that is positive?

The less sense it makes, the more applicable it is to management.

Now why would management want to listen to the employees?

You get more truthful answers from a Magic 8 Ball than you do from management.

I don't make the rules, I just break them.

Is stupidity replacing common sense?

In most businesses, shouldn't management be called mismanagement?

The attempts at remakes of some of the songs from the '60s and '70s are sacrilege.

Karma's a bitch that needs to visit some people more often.

Maybe the reason why so many Karen's get visited by karma is because opposites attract.

I wonder if karma has a naughty-and-nice list like Santa.

Not much is more satisfying than seeing the look of shock on an entitled person's face when you tell them "No."

Please don't speak your mind, it's a terrible thing to waste.

If you offer me a penny for my thoughts, don't be offended when I give you my two cents' worth.

Maybe the grass on the other side of the fence is greener because it's artificial turf.

Some of the Disney classics make me think the writers and animators were paid with drugs.

Ever wonder what a songwriter was going through when they wrote some of their songs?

Why do retail jobs feel like one of those hidden camera shows?

Is there a difference between gibberish and nonsensical? Management usually seems too fluent in both.

What do joggers/bikers have against using the paths designated for them? Are they trying to get run over?

Work is like a vampire; it sucks the life right out of you.

Are we sure the zombie apocalypse isn't happening with the government already? Most of them seem to be brainless.

I keep catching myself telling my blind dog to watch where she's going or to look out.

Kerfuffle sounds like something Dr. Seuss should have made up.

Wine makes me happy; you not so much.

Three branches of government, three rings in a circus. Coincidence, you be the judge.

With the terms and conditions some wireless and/or Internet providers require, they may as well claim your firstborn.

A singing competition, except it's with only misheard lyrics.

If I start making sense, get me to a doctor.

Working in customer service for so long has definitely awakened my inner cynic.

I shouldn't have to be a contortionist to clean the inside of my windshield.

How do you emphasize sarcasm when using sign language?

Contradictions, double standards, hypocrisy, and corruption: the cornerstones of corporate America.

Telling my blind dog to watch out is as effective as telling my teenager to listen.

Why do mattress companies advertise people sleeping atop a bare mattress? Who does that?

With a national debt of $34 trillion, what kind of credit score does the government have?

If you miss a sale on a car or a mattress, don't worry, they'll be on sale again next week.

The Star Wars environment on the planets on the outer rim looks like the Wild West with technology.

When I had my dog Snickers neutered, should I have changed his name to Milky Way?

Alzheimer's disease is a terrible thing, but at least you can make new friends every day.

If your partner/significant other says they want to spice things up, they don't mean using seasonings.

Which is better, to know a lot about a little or to know a little about a lot?

The unwritten rule of corporate America: us vs. them = hourly vs. salary.

I refuse to age gracefully. I'm going to be like a hemorrhoid, forever a pain in your ass.

Kind of hard to follow the rules when they're constantly being changed.

Training seems to be an afterthought for most businesses.

What they lack in empathy, they make up for with incompetence.

If it wasn't/isn't management's idea, they don't like it.

After a day at work, all I need is sanity and a stiff drink.

Can someone invent the smell-o-vision already?

Oxymorons

Controlled chaos
Military intelligence
Jumbo shrimp
Honest politician
British comedy (with the exception of Monty Python)
Polite Karen
Competent management

Music Quotes / Movie References

There will definitely be more music references than movie references. That is because while I do watch movies, I listen to music more frequently.

Phil Collins wasn't kidding when he called this "the land of confusion."

Jim Morrison was spot on when said "people are strange."

Like Metallica said, "Ignorance and arrogance go in hand."

As Billy Joel said, "I'd rather laugh with the sinners than cry with the saints, the sinners are much more fun."

Axl Rose asked a really good question when he said, "What's so civil about war anyway?"

Did the people who developed AI not see *The Terminator* and learn anything about Skynet?

Hallmark channel is great at recycling. Same plot rewritten eight different ways year after year for Christmas movies.

John Lennon sure had a very active imagination. Just listen to "Imagine," some of those ideas are unattainable.

Taking a ride on the Crazy Train sounds like a good time.

The song "Santa Claus Is Coming to Town" makes Santa sound like a stalker.

Living like a Hobbit sounds like it would be nice—food, wine, and communing with nature.

It would probably be a bad idea for Tom Petty and The Heartbreakers and Sgt. Peppers Lonely Hearts Club Band to meet each other.

When Metallica said "Hearing only you want to hear and knowing only what you heard," they pretty much defined selective hearing.

I wonder how much Led Zepplin thinks the "Stairway to Heaven" costs.

Robert Plant wasn't kidding when in "Stairway to Heaven," he said, "'Cause you know sometimes words have two meanings."

Jon Bon Jovi was right when in "Wanted Dead or Alive," he said, "Sometimes you tell the day by the bottle that you drink."

Do the "Highway to Hell" and the "highway to the danger zone" ever intersect?

Van Halen was on to something when they wrote "Running with the Devil." That sounds like fun.

When Billy Joel said "Don't argue with a crazy man," he was right. It could also apply to a smart-ass.

When Rockwell wrote "Somebody's Watching Me," I bet they had no idea how true it would become.

Considering his history with kids, "Pretty Young Thing" wasn't the best idea for a song by Michael Jackson.

In every delivery room, they should be playing "Push It" by Salt-N-Pepa in the background.

Every guilty verdict should play "The End of the Innocence" by Don Henley.

In "Indian Reservation (The Lament of the Cherokee Reservation Indian)" by Paul Revere and the Raiders, when they say "But maybe someday when they learn, Cherokee nation will return," they fail to realize "they" will never learn.

The bass line in "Imagine" would be great in a fishing game.

In "Comfortably Numb," I wonder if Pink Floyd was being rhetorical when they asked, "Is there anybody out there"?

When Alice Cooper wrote "Poison," did he know that poison and venom are different things?

In "Come Together," when The Beatles says "He got feet down below his knees," the only thing I can think of is, *Well, I hope so.*

In "Final Countdown," when Europe asked, "Will things ever be the same again?" the answer is "No, no, they will not.

Lit was right when they said, "I am my own worst enemy."

Let's hope the "Message in the Bottle" the police sent out wasn't asking about your car's extended warranty.

When Men at Work asked "Who can it be now?" did they really want to know?

If I gave all my secrets away like One Republic says, I'd have to be committed.

I wonder what it is that Meatloaf won't do for love.

I guess since Billy Joel didn't start the fire is why Bruce Springsteen is "Dancing in the Dark."

Does The Beatles' "Long and Winding Road" lead to Lynyrd Skynyrd's "Sweet Home Alabama" or Guns N' Roses's "Paradise City"?

I wonder why Tears for Fears thinks "Everybody Wants to Rule the World."

In "Crazy Train," Ozzy Osbourne says, "I listen to preachers, I listen to fools." I only wonder "what's the difference."

In "Learning to Fly," when Tom Petty said "What goes up must come down," I thought to myself, *Yeah, that's pretty much how gravity works.*

How does ZZ Top know that every girl is crazy for a "Sharp Dressed Man"?

If hell is within the planet, how is it supposed to "Rain like hell from above" like Billy Idol said in "Rebel Yell"?

For the opening line of "Rock of Ages," Def Leppard should have used the Swedish Chef from The Muppets.

What if instead of driving a Chevy to the levee, you drove a Ford to a fjord or a Ram to a dam?

Bill Withers's "Lean on Me" should be a good song for the first dance at a wedding.

In "Freeway of Love," Aretha Franklin makes herself sound like a Mary Kay Cosmetics top salesperson when she talks about a pink Cadillac.

I agree with Bob Seger when he said, "I like that old-time rock and roll."

The Doobie Brothers gave some good advice when they said, "Whoa, listen to the music."

Why, yes, Creedence Clearwater Revival, I have seen the rain coming down on a sunny day.

Hey, Duran Duran, is there really an "Ordinary World"?

In "Wonderwall," when Oasis says "And all the lights that lead us there are blinding," they obviously were using LED lights.

I like how The Byrds wrote an entire song ("Turn! Turn! Turn!") about Newton's third law—for every action, there is an equal and opposite reaction.

Whether they know it or not, Nirvana gave some good advice for the kitchen when they said, "Take your time hurry up" in "Come as You Are."

If thunder is just a noise, what does AC/DC mean when they say thunderstruck?

Profound Thoughts

Sometimes while doing even the most mundane things, these thoughts that make me stop and say "Wow" just pop into my head.

What other world do otherworldly possessions come from?

Cancer brings sorrow, sorrow brings darkness, darkness brings death. Yearn to be a beacon of light in a time of darkness.

If blue is associated with being sad, then why is there the blue bird of happiness?

If God is so good, how come so many people are raised to be God-fearing?

Life is like a jukebox set on random, you never know what's coming up next.

Those who view themselves as "God's gift to the world" are the quickest to pass blame and play victim.

Usually, those who speak the loudest have the least to say.

Do EMTs travel in teams of two because they are a "pair-of-medics"?

If everyone is okay with eating the "mascot" of Thanksgiving (i.e., turkey) on Thanksgiving, how come no one eats rabbit on Easter?

If we're supposed to learn from our mistakes, shouldn't we as a species be smarter than we are?

So women get offended that men only look at their chests then turn around and wear shirts that draw attention to their chests.

The path to Easy Street is laden with potholes, wrong turns, and road construction.

We may never know who wrote some of the best lines from presidential speeches since they have an entire staff that do nothing but write stuff the president gets credit for.

Cliché Statements

We all know these. They've been around for so long they've just become included in our everyday thoughts and conversations.

That's like trying to fit a square peg in a round hole.

You can pick your nose, you can pick your friends, but can't pick your friend's nose.

Laughter is the best medicine.

Old habits die hard.

The truth hurts.

Working hard or hardly working.

You can sleep when you're dead.

Work smarter, not harder.

You can't fix stupid.

The asylum is run by the inmates.

Why do hot dogs come in packs of ten, but hot dog rolls only come in packs of eight?

Stupidity knows no bounds.

All dressed up and nowhere to go.

Slow and steady wins the race.

The Art of Aging

Unfortunately, aging is something that no one can escape. Being a member of Gen X, I'm reminded on almost a daily basis that even the best (or worst) of us is getting older.

Gen X has some of the most iconic cinematic music—that is, Star Wars and Indiana Jones.

It takes a lot to offend those of us from Gen X. We grew up drinking water from the hose and watching a cross-dressing rabbit sing opera.

The older I get, the earlier I get tired.

The older I get, the earlier it gets late.

As I get older, the less entertaining a night on the town sounds.

I do a much better imitation of Rice Krispies as I get older.

The less I do, the more tired I get.

I'm not getting old; I'm aging with style.

Growing up, we were always told don't talk to strangers. Guess that means I shouldn't talk to myself; doesn't get much stranger than that.

Kitchen Humor

I've been working in kitchens for more than twenty years. Sure, not all the humor is appropriate, but occasionally, you get one of those jokes that is both comical and not rated R. Sometimes the jokes can be so corny that they give dad jokes a run for their money.

If edamame, who's the daddy?

There's no bitchin' in the kitchen.

There's no need for tattoos when you've got scars from cuts and burns.

If you've got time to lean, you've got time to clean.

I've been in kitchens for over twenty years, and I've never heard anyone say "If you can't handle the heat, get out of the kitchen." I guess it's something Hollywood came up with.

Political Mumbo Jumbo

Politicians talk so much crap I bet their breath stinks.

Marjorie Taylor Greene is like that crazy aunt everybody has something to say about but nobody will.

When I heard that Trump was now selling Bibles, my first thought was his version was going to portray him as the savior, and my second thought was he was only going to publish Revelations.

I think the comment I saw said politicians are like diapers, usually full of shit and need to be changed often.

Imagine the size of Trump's nose if, like Pinocchio, it grew every time he lied.

Political amnesia—forgetting all the bad a politician did previously and trying to reelect them.

Biden needs to have his political headquarters at a nursing home.

With so many domestic problems (i.e., homelessness, health care costs, etc.), why does the government keep sending money overseas?

The same way they bleep language on TV, they should do to Trump when he lies.

Regardless of who is elected president, a new position will need to be created. For Biden, a geriatric nurse, for Trump, a parole officer.